Gerald,
Wishing you Easter Blessings!
Love,
Mary Lou & Tom
Easter, 2010

Cloister Cats

Other books by Richard Surman available from Collins

Cathedral Cats
Church Cats
Dog Collar

Cloister Cats

Richard Surman

Collins

Collins

a division of HarperCollins Publishers

77–85 Fulham Palace Road, London w6 8jb

www.collins.co.uk

First published in Great Britain in 2007 by
HarperCollins Publishers

1

A catalogue record for this book is available from the British Library.

isbn-13 978-0-00-723210-9

Design by Susie Bell

Printed and bound in Hong Kong by Printing Express

Collins

Contents

Introduction

Cloister Cats are, on the whole, modest creatures: eschewing the high profile of Cathedral Cats, Cloister Cats do not bask in public view, neither do they get much attention from the public, for the simple reason that by the very nature of the cats' surroundings, they are set apart.

The cloister cats featured in this book live in very distinctive surroundings: some live in monasteries with fine traditional cloisters – others are part of communities that remain entirely set apart from the outside world. Yet others live in places that only used to be monastic buildings. But for the most part they are united in the sense of being part of a community in which there is an element of religious seclusion and contemplation. The places in which they live are extraordinarily varied; from modest surroundings like St Monica's Priory in London's Hoxton, to the grandeur of Mottisfont and Forde Abbey, and from the rural simplicity of Holy Hill Hermitage to the antiquity of Iona: places as different as the cats who live in them.

Many of the cats featured herein are foundlings, who, like pilgrims of old seeking sanctuary, have come in need of help, shelter, food or companionship (and sometimes all four). Often the cats have chosen the communities. Others, Leo at Blackfriars in Cambridge for example, have been sought out by the community. Other cats have arrived at a community with their human companions, like Bonnie at Walsingham Priory, and Splash at the Iona Community.

Life in a religious community can be very intense. Pressures of harmonious co-existence, of following vows of obedience, chastity and poverty, all have to be dealt with. Looking in from outside, many people have a rather rosy perception of the monastic religious life, but in some ways it must be pretty tough. Maybe that is why the cloister cat has such a major place in the affections of many religious communities in this country. One of the monks at Glenstal Abbey commented wryly to me that 'Monks need cats, to remind them not to be catty'. In some communities, particularly those with nursing or care activities, their cats have brought great pleasure to the sick and the elderly. Oscar, at St John's in Oxford, even gets to ride on an elderly lady's electric wheelchair, to the delight of the all the residents. There is no rule that forbids a moment's happiness, and for many people, the opportunity to stroke a cat, to spend a moment playing with one of these graceful and quixotic creatures, is an opportunity to take a moment out of the rough and tumble of everyday life, be it in monastic or secular surroundings.

Finding the cats portrayed in this book wasn't easy. By definition they were not well-known, and I am grateful to the many people who gave me leads and suggestions that sometimes did, and sometimes

LEFT
Oscar of St John's, All Saints Convent
ABOVE
The sign on the library door at
Alnmouth Priory

didn't, lead to discovering a cloister cat. There are
many others whose help with this book was invaluable,
in particular my editors Ian Metcalfe and Fiona
Tucker at Collins, and my wife Blanca, without whose
encouragement, and patience with my frequent
absences, I could not have completed Cloister Cats.
Finally I would like to express my appreciation and
thanks to all the communities featured, for the
kind and warm hospitality that was invariably
extended to me.

Brother Pascal, the Guardian of Alnmouth Friary,
summed up the spirit of Cloister Cats, in his account
of the two Friary cats Agnes and Clare:

'For 35 years Alnmouth Friary has been giving food
and shelter to homeless men, "wayfarers" as we still
call them in the Order, so it was natural for us to
welcome Clare and Agnes, two rejected homeless
kittens, into our midst! These two sisters, half Siamese,
were "rescued" from life "on the road".'

For Blanca

Agnes
Society of St Francis, Alnmouth Friary

'May Thou be praised, my Lord, with all
Thy creatures.'

From The Canticle of Brother Son, St Francis of Assisi

The Northumberland coastline is dramatic and
beautiful, but Brother Edward, who has been at the
friary since its founding, told me that the climate
varies from Mediterranean at best to Arctic rather too
often – and he vividly remembers the bitter cold of the
early days, when the friars slept on the floor in a house
that had become near-derelict.

For many years the friary maintained the tradition of
giving food and shelter to homeless men, known to
the Franciscans as 'wayfarers'; these days, the friars
offer hospitality, retreats and day visits to those who
want time out from the pressures of the outside world,
and annually receive over a thousand staying guests,
and many more who visit for the day. With such a

HISTORY

Alnmouth Friary was given to the Franciscan Friars in
1961. A rambling, late Victorian building set in
extensive gardens, it overlooks Alnmouth village and
the wild beauty of the Northumbrian coast. The
surrounding area is steeped in early Christian history:
St. Cuthbert was elected bishop here, and just up the
coast lies the holy island of Lindisfarne.

tradition of hospitality and shelter-giving, it was only natural for the friars to welcome into their midst two homeless half-Siamese kittens. They were named after St Clare of Assisi and her sister, St Agnes of Assisi, two great followers of St Francis, who lived the contemplative life in the cloister of San Damiano in Assisi.

Clare, who died two years ago, was very much the 'Abbess' and had a very definite presence, but she was also very trusting and affectionate and would hop onto any lap, willing or unwilling. 'Here I am,' she would insist, 'this is what you have been waiting for.' But she was always appreciative of those who held doors open for her, and would show her thanks with little purrs and noises. Both brothers and guests would 'melt' in her presence and to tired and stressed retreatants her presence would help them unwind and relax.

Clare also had an appetite sufficient for both cats; cake was her abiding passion, and she'd turn seductive blue eyes on anyone who was about to tuck into a piece of homemade cake. The brothers took to warning guests that they had two options with a slice of cake: eat it quickly, or lose it. But above all she was good company, and would run to greet the brethren, tail hoisted and hooked in enthusiastic greeting, as they returned from work. Brother Paschal, the Guardian of the friary, found her a wonderful companion at times of stress or worry.

Agnes is a shyer cat, and the general opinion is that she was overshadowed by Clare. Clearly Clare was more energetic: she was a good soccer player, while Agnes likes extremes of comfort, lolling around on chairs, disappearing up the sleeves of brothers' habits, making surprise appearances on guests' beds. She also surprises guests and brothers alike, as she will often slip into a room, settle down to sleep unseen, then wake up the hapless occupant of the room at about 3am with an imperious tap of her paw in order that the door can be opened to let her out.

There are other possible causes for Agnes's reticence, and one of them has to do with Dexter, a bouncing Norfolk terrier who belongs to Stephen, a volunteer and highly gifted gardener. Dexter normally keeps watch in the drive, placing himself in the centre of the driveway, wagging his tail wildly at cars that are vainly trying to get past. Dexter has a trick up his sleeve: he has discovered Agnes's cat flap. Poor Agnes – no wonder she's a bit reticent about using use her cat flap, as she often finds Dexter's head poking through it, panting eagerly at her. Since Clare's sad demise, Agnes has shown a desire to be more centre stage; one Easter Brother Paschal was drawing breath to sing the Magnificat, when Agnes hopped up beside him, and mewed loudly.

Like Clare before her, Agnes waits outside the kitchen, knowing never to cross the line with a paw, but she is much more picky with her food. And she follows the brothers around, sitting on their work when they are trying to write at the desk. Her disconcerting habit of walking on the phone, thus cutting people off mid-call, is the only habit that is vigorously discouraged. St Francis used to call all creatures his 'Brother' or 'Sister', and Brother Paschal reflects that 'Here in this Franciscan Friary we know this to be a living reality, and Clare and Agnes have helped us to rejoice and delight in all God's creatures'.

OPENING PAGE

In the friary garden

RIGHT

Clare does not like closed windows or doors

Millie
Anglican Order of St Benedict, Alton Abbey

'As cellarer of the monastery let there be chosen from the community one who is wise, of mature character, sober, not a great eater, not haughty, not excitable.'

From the Rule of St Benedict

The Times described Alton Abbey as 'the best kept secret in the Church of England' – thus possibly turning it into the worst kept secret in the Church of England! A casual glimpse of the Rhenish 'pepper pot' tower of the abbey church through the trees is almost enough to persuade oneself that one is in Normandy: this striking building, set in some 80 acres of woodland, was designed by Sir Charles Nicholson, and built by the monks themselves in the late nineteen hundreds to accommodate retired seamen.

It was the retirement of a vicar of St Paul's Knightsbridge that caused the community to adopt its first cat. When the vicar was making arrangements for his retirement, he asked Abbot Giles if the community

HISTORY
Alton Abbey, an Anglican Benedictine monastery, is an architectural gem set discreetly amidst the beech woods of Hampshire. Originally its purpose was to care for retired merchant seamen – the community came about through the missionary work of Father Charles Hopkins among merchant seamen in foreign ports; its work is now centred on prayer, running retreats, giving lectures, baking bread and the manufacture of incense.

would look after his cat Misty for a couple of months. But Misty made herself rather more at home than was intended, and ended up living at Alton Abbey for nine years. Then one damp November day, the feast day of St Gertrude (who is variously described as the patron saint of cats and of those who fear mice), a young cat turned up at the door of the abbey. She rolled over disingenuously at the feet of the Abbot and Prior, flashed a few appealing looks, got fed, and promptly disappeared. The fleeting visitor hadn't gone far, however. She haunted the woods adjacent to the monastery, appearing at odd times asking to be fed, and as time passed, her disappearances became less frequent, until she finally decided that she would move in. And once that decision had been taken, Millie declared her annexation of the monastery in short order. One near victim of this fierce territoriality was a visiting blind priest's guide dog. For the whole of his visit Millie sat growling on the inside of the enclosure door, which was thankfully kept firmly closed. She didn't endear herself to the guest master either, having given him a sharp nip when he picked her up: it says something for the Benedictine spirit of hospitality that she wasn't shown the door permanently.

Millie has an aversion to closed doors: an early sortie into the abbey church while the monks were at their offices caused much distraction and hilarity, and resulted in a ban from any further church attendance. So closed doors represent a challenge that Millie is forever trying to overcome. One welcoming door is that of the abbey bakery, and another that of the guest house, through which Millie charms her way in order to shamelessly solicit attention from visitors and guests.

Millie's real nest is in Abbot Giles's study, where a cosy fire and comfortable bed are at hand, as is a doorway to the grounds through which she can come and go as she pleases. And somewhere in the background lurks the call of the wild. For she came from the woods, and when one sees her spread-eagled on the trunk of a tree, it is quite clear that the woodland environment is where she feels at her wildest best. Millie pelts across the open spaces between trees, scaling them in a frenzy of excitement, ending up teetering crazily on a narrow branch, looking around with startled eyes and flattened ears, before dashing down again to join in mortal combat with a wind-blown leaf or two.

The monastery has a pond which is home to a vast number of large frogs. I don't know what it is about cats and frogs. The cats obviously enjoy stalking the frogs, but rarely seem to know what to do once they are actually nose to nose with one. And recently the tables turned. It was a warm day, and Millie was lying in the shade of tree by the pond. Nearby was a small, and apparently confused frog, which decided to hop onto Millie's back. She was later spotted, complete with inscrutable amphibian passenger jogging on her back, oblivious to the hitchhiker's presence.

OPENING PAGE
Millie at her best in wild woodland
LEFT
On the way to the abbey bakery
BELOW
Watching for wind-blown leaves

Inky
Poor Clare Monastery, Arkley

'Let the porteress be mature in her manner of acting, discerning, and of a suitable age. Let her remain in an open cell without a door during the day.'

From the Rule of St Clare

When Sister Bernadette, the porteress at the Poor Clare Monastery in Arkley, opened the door to me, I told her that I had an appointment to see Inky, the community's cat. She goggled at me, and shut the door firmly in my face. Luckily Sister Francesca, the monastery cook, and Inky's keeper, had been listening out for my arrival, and came to the rescue.

Inky's arrival at the monastery of the Poor Clares in Barnet, North London, is a tale of Dickensian poignancy. On a bitterly cold Christmas Day, with an iron hard frost and cold wind sweeping in from nearby fields, Sister Francesca was busy preparing the festive lunch for the whole community. Looking out of the kitchen window, she spotted an unkempt and

HISTORY

The Poor Clares in Arkley make their living from the sales of homemade marmalade and jam. This seems to be something of a speciality in the English order of Poor Clares, and a very successful one. They also make church linen, church candles and greeting cards – a hive of cottage industry. The community moved here in 1970, and an important aspect of their work is in running retreats for people who live in parishes within the Diocese of Westminster.

in horror. When she opened them again, the birds had scattered in alarm, and Inky was ravenously tucking into the breadcrumbs. A tin of sardines was found and opened, and placed out on the grass – but Inky had disappeared like a shot at the first sound of a door being opened. After a while she emerged again, nose uplifted and twitching: she crept over to the opened tin, looked around, and dived face first into her first ever Christmas delicacy as if she was trying to get inside the tin. No one can recall when the transition between Inky the furtive visitor and Inky the resident took place. She had been eating all the food put outside for her, and then suddenly she was inside. Inky took a further three months to become at all sociable with Sister Francesca – but now clambers up onto her lap. She has realised whose hand it is that wields the can opener.

underfed black cat, looking out from under a nearby bush at one of the bird tables that the sisters maintain. Followers of St Francis and St Clare have a particular affection for animals – though more than one person has commented, rather unfairly I think, that if St Francis had really cared for birds, he might have done better to preach to cats!

Sister Francesca was concerned for the cat, though also for the birds that were busily feeding at a pile of breadcrumbs that she had put out earlier. She was on the verge of going to find something to eat for this poor Christmas orphan of a cat, when to her horror she saw the cat streak across the open lawn. Reaching the bird table, he leapt up; thinking that the cat was after one of the birds, Sister Francesca closed her eyes

The work of the Poor Clares at Arkley is chiefly that of prayer. Following austere rules, the whole community meets at midnight for Matins (although an exception is made for Inky), and then rises for the day at 5.30am – although nobody can persuade a sleeping cat to get up against its will, without resorting to force or violent noise of some kind – behaviour that would be unseemly and out of place for the Poor Clares. However, Sister Francesca has encouraged Inky's compliance in this case by feeding her at 5.30am. Inky has some odd rituals too: on regular walks with Sister Francesca, Inky will accompany her on a long circular path. She'll go round this three times only. Then she

goes to the centre point of the circular walk, slowly rotates on the spot, and then rejoins Sister Francesca on the path, and walks in exactly the opposite direction, three times only. Perhaps it is as Garrison Keillor once commented, 'Cats are intended to show us that not everything in nature has a purpose'.

I was curious about Saint Clare. 'Whose patron saint is she?' I asked Sister Francesca. I was told that she is the patron saint of television production, and shares the job with the archangel Gabriel. The story of how she came to be the patron saint of such a modern and thoroughly secular medium is that Clare was in very poor health, which prevented her from being moved from her sick bed to the chapel even for Midnight Mass at Christmas. In despair at being unable to attend the mass, she lay back in her bed, and gazing at the wall, she saw an image form, of the mass that was being celebrated some way off. But I don't think this means that watching television is generally accepted as offering similar spiritual benefits to partaking in the Mass!

OPENING PAGE

Inky: the cat who came in from the cold

FAR LEFT

Inky likes to walk with Sister Francesca

LEFT

A cat that prefers the company of the sisters

Blackie
Anglican Order of St Benedict, Burford Priory

'In the reception of the poor and of pilgrims the greatest care and solicitude should be shown, because it is especially in them that Christ is received.'

On the reception of guests, from the Rule of St Benedict

The first major rebuilding of Burford Priory after the dissolution of the monasteries took place in the early 17th century, when Laurence Tanfield, a barrister and MP, acquired the property. The second period of modernization was during the occupancy of William Lenthall, one-time Speaker in Parliament. Clearly a man of oscillating loyalties during the time of the Civil War, he was a signatory to the death warrant of Charles I, but then promoted the restoration of the monarchy. In the 19th century John Lenthall, faced with a decline in family fortunes, had more than half of the old building demolished, and it decayed gently until Colonel de Sales la Terriere and his wife carried out major restoration work at the beginning of the 20th century.

HISTORY

Burford Priory, unusually, returned to monastic use after an interval of some 400 years in private ownership. A religious house existed here from the 13th century – probably Augustinian canons, whose duties included the running of a hospital. There are traces of the old building in the present-day priory, despite substantial remodelling and rebuilding over the centuries when it was a private home, until it became a community again in the middle of the 20th century.

Then in 1948 a community of sisters based near Oxford, who were looking for a place where they could lead an enclosed contemplative community life, following the Benedictine Rule, happened on the Priory. In the 1960s the rule of strict enclosure was relaxed, and eventually the novitiate was opened to men. The present community of eleven is now mixed, and divides its time between work, prayer, study and hospitality.

There has been a cat at Burford Priory since 1970, when the community took in a stray with an injured back leg. The second cat to arrive was Suki, brought to the Priory by the widow of a retired local doctor. Suki quickly endeared herself to Sister Mary Bernard, by

clambering up her habit and settling immovably on her lap. She enjoyed a long and tranquil life there from 1978 to 1991. Then came Vosgi: a real community cat, he took over the whole building, roaming jovially from room to room, hogging the best place in front of the parlour fireplace during the winter, and continually trying to gain access to the kitchen – in the spirit of friendship for the brothers and sisters working in the kitchen, rather than out of interest in food, naturally!

Blackie is the present community cat, who arrived in 2005. She had previously belonged to a Greek hairdresser whose wife had become allergic to cat fur;

so from a rather chic 'salon de coiffure', Blackie then found herself in very different surroundings. She is rather a grand cat, more used to the scent of hairspray and pomade than rigours of community life, and thoroughly resistant to the allure of the Priory's wild woodland. It certainly took some time for Blackie to settle in: carefully guarding a pink ball that was her treasure, she was very wary of this radical change of environment, and for a while all that could be seen of her was a pair of startled eyes staring from the undergrowth in the garden, or from deep in the shadows in the priory entrance hall. But both the present Abbot, Father Stuart, and Sister Mary Bernard, devoted a great deal of time and patience in encouraging Blackie to be more at ease, and little by little she came out of her shell.

Now she counts off the community as they come down the stairs to the chapel, and is frequently to be found curled up contentedly on Sister Mary Bernard's bed. She also tries in vain to get access to the refectory during meal times, and the readings are punctuated by plaintive high-pitched pleas for admission from the old cloister gardens.

Of course, now that she is acclimatised, the Priory grounds are a delight: Blackie enjoys sitting on the banks of the river Windrush, as it winds its way gently through the grounds. She gazes at her own reflection as if thinking that she really ought to do something about her hair.

OPENING PAGE
Blackie enjoys the tranquility of the Priory
LEFT
A cat who likes to keep her hair neat
BELOW
Blackie enjoys the warmth of the
parlour fireplace

Leo
The Order of Preachers, Blackfriars Cambridge

'The main purpose for you having come together is to live harmoniously in your house, intent upon God in oneness of mind and heart.'

From the Rule of St Augustine, adopted by St Dominic

Lion, Lion burning bright
In the Library by night!
Soppy and demanding Beast,
Slow to hunt, and swift to feast:
Lion, Lion, burning bright –
Please don't give us such a fright!
To the tune of Petra

Few cats can claim to be celebrated in doggerel, but the Dominican cat Leo, a rather aristocratic Birman, had the misfortune to be nudged too close to the Old Library fireplace one evening as a visitor inadvertently stepped back onto him. A flaming Leo was hastily extinguished, with no lasting ill effects, but the event was deemed sufficiently dramatic to warrant a

HISTORY

The first Dominican presence in Cambridge is recorded in the 13th century, when the principal activities were writing and teaching, although the friars also served the day to day parochial needs of the ordinary people of Cambridge. After the dissolution parts of the church were 'recycled' in the buttery, hall and fellows' parlour of Emmanuel College. The Dominicans returned to Cambridge in the 1930s with the generous gift of a fine Italianate house which is now deemed a domus scriptorum, a 'house of writers'.

commemorative verse by the present Prior of Black-friars. Not that Leo was any stranger to adventure: some while before the library fire, he got trapped on the second floor of a neighbouring building that was in the process of being demolished. On discovering his whereabouts, the Friars, armed with the longest ladder they could lay their hands on, invaded the building site and swarmed up the ladder, habits flapping in the wind, in a valiant if somewhat wobbly rescue bid. An unrepentant Leo was brought down, his ash blond fur stained a rusty red from brick dust.

Though there was a Dominican priory in Cambridge from the 13th century, Tudor religious policy brought an abrupt halt to this in 1538, when the house was surrendered to the crown. The Dominicans did not return to Cambridge until the 1930s, through a generous gift from Enrichetta Bullough, in the form of an elegant Italianate house designed by Cambridge architect H.C. Hughes; after the death of her husband she had found the house too large and lonely. Now this 'house of writers' offers a haven for the friars to develop their learned theological and literary studies along with administering a 'novitiate' for other priories within the English Dominican Province.

Cats have been a feature of Blackfriars in Cambridge since the mid 1940s, though not without some

controversy (as befits an academic institution). When Leo's predecessor Squeaky died, the then Prior announced that there should be no more cats. A flurry of discussion and academic deliberation within the community followed this edict, and the conclusion was that such a decision could only be arrived at by community consensus. Feelings ran high, to the extent that the Prior was briefly 'sent to Coventry'. Eventually a compromise was arrived at. There could be another cat, on condition that he or she would have to await the end of the long university vacation, and that said cat would under no circumstances come to the part of the Priory where the Prior lived. (Quite how one explains that to a cat I can't imagine. They pride them-

selves on being oblivious to any instruction or rule.) Then there was the matter of choosing the replacement: Father Aidan wanted a long-haired cat, while Father Richard, now Regent of Blackfriars Oxford, was insistent on a short-haired one. More heated academic debate raged as to the merits of both types, much to the delight of the Prior, who exploited the differences of opinion as a sign that a cat would be divisive. The obvious settlement was agreed upon – a semi-long-haired, or semi-short-haired cat (depending on which side of the argument you stood) would be found. Father Aidan suggested a Birman, and so a breeder was found, deep in the Fens, who could fulfil the Friars' requirement for a suitable cat. But then

came the problem of how to get the cat: the only person in the Priory to hold a driver's licence was the Prior, and he wasn't about to drive around the Fens in search of a remote cattery. In the event a Fellow of Trinity College came to the rescue, and so Leo was installed at Blackfriars.

My impression is that from the outset, Leo made no attempt to accommodate the differing sensitivities of the community. Indeed his pranks seemed almost designed to taunt those who disapproved of his presence. As a young kitten, he habitually perched on the head of a statue of St Dominic on the main stairway, responding cheerfully to the greetings of those who appreciated his presence, and glaring balefully at those who shuddered in displeasure at the sight of a cat. He got to know the chapel too, where he pushed his luck rather, even with his most ardent admirers. His first chapel appearance was during a sermon given by a visiting American Dominican. The sermon was peppered with a number of humorous points: that the congregation laughed at all the wrong times, the preacher put down to the oddness of English university humour. What he didn't realise was that Leo was peeping out from under the altar frontal, and stealing the whole show. Leo couldn't get enough of the chapel: he'd wander in during vespers, and always shot in ahead of any visiting priest. Eventually even the cat lovers of the community agreed that Leo was going too far; his continual fondness for concealment under the altar frontal eventually proved too much: the only sign of his presence would be when a paw would sneak out from under the altar frontal, flapping around in an attempt to catch the hem of a celebrant's vestments.

Leo's banishment from the chapel, unacceptable and incomprehensible in his eyes, has had other and equally distracting consequences, for now Leo stands outside the chapel door and meows bitterly in protest at his exclusion. But apart from his obvious displeasure at the chapel ban, Leo is a cat at peace with himself and his surroundings. He makes himself fully at home in the extensive New Library, where he can often be found dozing on a sunny window ledge, and can depend on a cheerful welcome to the novices' rooms, , where his favourite spots can be detected in the shallow depressions left on bed covers and armchairs, and indeed to the room of the present Prior. His unfortunate brush with fire has had little effect on his love of intense heat, and he still stretches out in front of the open fire in the Old Library, but a little bit further back than before the conflagration, to allow him a safer escape route from the careless heel of a chance visitor.

OPENING PAGE
The patrician Leo
PREVIOUS PAGE, LEFT
Leo, working in the library
PREVIOUS PAGE, RIGHT
Leo, still working in the library
RIGHT
A moment of spring sun in the garden

Tamar
Community of the Holy Name, Derby

'Let them sleep clothed and girded with belts or cords – but not with their knives at their sides, lest they cut themselves in their sleep.'
On how the Sisters should sleep, from the Rule of St Benedict

When the Community of the Holy Name moved from Malvern to Derby, two cats – Ben and Benji – came along to help them settle in. But time and illness eventually took their toll on the cats, and Sister Brenda, gardener and 'cat warden', faced with the melancholy prospect of a catless community, contacted the Cats Protection League, to see if they had a suitable candidate. 'Well, yes', came the hesitant reply, 'but he's a bit timid'. Sister Brenda decided to go ahead, and after about two weeks, Tamar arrived, aged two and a half months, and a bundle of nerves. For a few weeks Tamar did nothing except lie under a table in the laundry, staring out in alarm if anyone so much as passed by.

HISTORY
Faced with a decline in numbers, in 1990 the sisters of the Community of the Holy Name decided to move their mother house from Malvern to Derby. The community, although dimished in size, still comprises about 25 sisters and novices, and to assist with the care of some of the older and less able sisters, there is also a small nursing staff, as well as a cook and two assistant gardeners.

Sister Brenda wondered whether the cat was ever going to emerge, but wisely left him undisturbed, busying herself in the extensive gardens. After a while Tamar did start to venture out, but only to accompany Sister Brenda round the convent at 5am, as she opened up the downstairs doors. And even then he'd jump in fright at an unexpected shadow or sharp sound.

Slowly, very slowly, he got more used to the day-to-day activity of the convent: his first real foray was into the nurses' sitting room – also used as a studio for those members of the community who enjoy painting and drawing, where his tentative attempts to socialise were somewhat frustrated by his habit of nibbling at the loose pages of crosswords left lying around. With a bit of delicate training, Tamar learned not to chew interesting pieces of paper, or pages in open books, and was allowed to become a regular fixture of the nurses' sitting room. By this time he had also started to join Sister Brenda on her early morning walk through the convent gardens. The gardens extend all round the convent buildings, and a series of paths winds through a fine collection of specimen trees: they often pause by the tree under which Benji was buried, and sometimes Sister Barbara is out there too, under another tree which she is equally certain is the one beneath which Benji lies.

Tamar's presence at the convent has inspired other cats to come calling, some with good intentions, and some less kindly disposed. Genghis, a battle-scarred bruiser from nearby, is one of the less welcome of Tamar's visitors: exploding through the cat flap, Genghis swept everything aside as he made straight for Tamar's food bowl, where he gobbled every last morsel while Tamar quivered behind the washing machine, hoping that Genghis wouldn't discover his hiding place.

A more benign visitor was Jamie – a stray in need of sanctuary. His trick was to clamber up into Sister Brenda's arms, and drape himself round her shoulders; he was eventually re-homed nearby. Nicodemus was another gentle stray, who eventually found a home with the convent cook – sensible fellow.

Tamar's objective in life remains to have as little disruption and drama as possible. He potters around after Sister Brenda, dozes in the greenhouse on the seed trays and listens to music in the evening. And when it's time for bed, he goes back to the safety of the laundry, where he has the choice of two accommodations, a comfortably lined summer basket, and a cosy 'igloo' bed for the winter, out of which he peers, looking like a wary feline totem figure.

Felix, Tinker and Mrs Tiggy
The Community of St Mary at the Cross, Edgware

'Before all things and above all things, care must be taken of the sick, so that they will be served as if they were Christ in person.'
On the sick, from the Rule of St Benedict

There are three cats and only three fully professed human members of the community, but though small in number, the Community of St Mary at the Cross, in North London's Edgware, is very much alive. Abbess Dame Mary Therese, Dame Barbara, and the recently fully professed Dame Mary Catherine are supported by some 15 oblates, and sustain a residential nursing home of some thirty residents and fifty staff, together with a retreat house and conference centre.

Ten cats in all are on the feline roll of honour at the convent, and the present trio, Felix, Tinker and Mrs Tiggy, are intricately integrated into the community and residential care home. Would that such effortless cohabitation extended to relations between the cats.

HISTORY

The Community of St Mary at the Cross was founded in 1866, and was originally based in East London. In the 1870s a rural site was acquired in Edgware (then in the depths of the countryside) and the convent was built containing a convalescent centre for sufferers of smallpox, which regularly swept through the poorer areas of London. The more recent buildings that house the residential care home came in the 1980s, when new social care legislation meant they had to build afresh, or close.

Mrs Tiggy is the senior of the three: she came of her own volition, having been literally 'left out in the cold' when her own family moved away. A Finnish oblate took her in, and in response to her twinkling eyes and winsome ways, named her Mrs Tiggy. At first the sisters were concerned that she might have another home in the vicinity, and toured the neighbourhood – with Mrs Tiggy tucked up contentedly in a pram – to see if she was recognised by anybody. Having satisfied themselves that she was indeed a stray, Mrs Tiggy was formally admitted to the convent, where she continued to sit expectantly in the pram, hoping in vain for further trips into the outside world. What the sisters did not know was that Mrs Tiggy was actually a most un-ladylike cat, and soon the peace of the enclosure was shattered by catcalls the like of which would have brought a blush to the cheeks of the toughest and roughest. Mrs Tiggy proved herself in fact an inner city pugilist with a most misleading name, with a rabid dislike of all cats, whether close by or in the far distance. Bluey, the resident Persian cat, was in no doubt as to Mrs Tiggy's character, and retreated from the scene.

Now, with the mellowing effect of time, Mrs Tiggy looks the picture of serenity, tucked up in her

conservatory basket. But when she and Tinker first came across each other, the ensuing battles reached Wagnerian proportions; which brings me to Tinker, a cat with an alarming interest in car mechanics.

His was another case of Sisters to the Rescue: one might think Edgware must be quite accustomed to the sight of Benedictine nuns – habits and cowls flying – rushing to the rescue of cats. Two sisters were queuing in their car at traffic lights in Edgware High Street, when Sister Barbara noticed to her horror a small cat clambering up onto the top of the wheel of the car in front. It disappeared into the wheel arch. Fearing the worst, both sisters leapt out of their car, one standing like a robed police officer with hands held high to stop all the traffic, while the other dashed to the car in front. The startled driver was ordered to stay put, while Sister Barbara groped around the back of the wheel, eventually emerging triumphantly with a small bedraggled tabby cat in her grasp. The sisters drove back to the convent with their new and rather bemused acquisition, who was named Tinker.

Mrs Tiggy was watching all the fuss over the new arrival from the shadows , and she was not pleased. Muttering unprintable threats, she bade her time until the courtyard was quiet – then waded into battle: the whole convent reverberated to the sounds of combat. After several weeks of conflict, with the sisters vainly trying to reach a peaceful solution, a sort of neutral zone was established, across which, from the safety of a

window, Tinker stared in angry reproach at Mrs Tiggy, who had to content herself with hurling insults in Tinker's direction.

Bluey had managed to stay clear of Mrs Tiggy's uncouth ways. But in due course he found his own paws full with the arrival of Felix.

Felix – like his cartoon namesake, a breezy and carefree cat – was brought to the convent by one of the gardeners; and he took an instant liking to Bluey. Unaware of the territorial problems, Felix strayed into Mrs Tiggy and Tinker's former combat zone. Mrs Tiggy was less of a problem: advancing years had slowed her down, and she was now content to walk stiffly to the conservatory door in order to mutter something unrepeatable at Tinker. Tinker however, illustrating how early experience can influence one's later behaviour, gave Felix an initial reception not unlike that given him by Mrs Tiggy when he first arrived: a few almighty spats ensued, and Felix retired in bewilderment to the safety of the enclosure, where he was consoled by Bluey. When Bluey developed cancer, Felix looked after him, and was distraught when he died. But Felix's good nature and chunky build kept him buoyant, and he strolls through the convent, tail held high in greeting. He ambles into the coffee room to mingle with visitors and volunteers, and nips in and out of chapel when he can. He has a thing about boxes too, and when passing an apparently empty box, Felix's head might just pop up in surprise greeting.

But my most abiding memory of the three cats is of the courtyard garden, with Mrs Tiggy squinting through the conservatory windows, Tinker glaring from under a wheelchair ramp, and Felix sniffing nonchalantly at a flower: a sort of 'High Noon' for cats, in the midst of suburban Edgware.

Tabitha Twitchit and Tilly
Forde Abbey (a former Cistercian monastery)

'The main purpose for you having come together is to live harmoniously in your house.'

From the Rule of St Augustine

Tabitha Twitchit and Tilly, like Murphy of Mottisfont, have strayed into this book under the category of 'living in a place that has cloisters'. They live in a remarkable family home, a former Cistercian monastery that passed by marriage into the Roper family at the beginning of the twentieth century. Thomas Chard's magnificent reconstruction of the abbey made it anything but a model of Cistercian austerity and led to its inclusion in Pevsner's *Hundred Best Buildings in England*.

Monastic life at Forde came to an abrupt halt at the dissolution, when the monastery was surrendered to the crown, and a second transformation of the former monastery took place in the 17th century, under the

HISTORY

Forde was one of a group of Cistercian foundations (Rievaulx and Fountains Abbeys being the most famous), all built to a common pattern. Thomas Chard, last abbot of Forde, reconstructed the abbey magnificently, and led Pevsner to include Forde in his *Hundred Best Buildings in England*. Remarkably, much of Abbot Chard's earlier work remains in the present building: the stately cloisters, the chapter house (now a chapel), kitchen and undercroft and the upper and lower refectories, to accommodate both vegetarian and meat-eating monks, each group disapproving of the other. Today Forde Abbey is a bustle of family life, centred around farming, opening the house to visitors, maintaining the extensive gardens, hosting weddings, and the recording of classical music.

direction of Edmund Prideaux, giving Forde Abbey much of its present form – though retaining some of the most significant elements of Abbot Chard's earlier work. Today's Forde Abbey is a bustle of family life, into which Tilly and Tabitha Twitchit had to fit as best they could. They had both come to the house without invitation, one from a stable where she had borne a litter of kittens, the other from who knows where.

This is principally a house of dogs – gun dogs mostly, who bustle and hustle around after one or other of the family, so with unfailing feline instinct, and a desire not to get trampled in the enthusiastic dog stampedes, Tabitha Twitchit attached herself to Heather the cook (and goes into a depression when cook goes away for her holidays). She also discovered the boiler room below stairs, and has a bed set next to a ground level window that allows her to observe outside comings and goings. In particular she keeps an eye out for any grandchildren, especially toddlers. Not that she wants to say 'hello': exactly the opposite. 'Goodbye, I'll be back when you've gone,' sums up both cats' attitude towards the very young.

Of the two, Tilly is the climber: her particular trick is to scale the walls until she reaches the Ropers' bedroom. Mr Roper is emphatic that he does not like cats, but I understand that when no one is looking he has quite a soft spot for Tilly. At least she is not summarily ejected from his bedroom window when she clambers in. Tabitha Twitchit tends to go her own way: she spends a lot of time in the gardens, making a brave show of stalking the proud roosters that strut around, until they get really close, a bit irritated, and start to stalk her. At which point discretion becomes the better part of valour, and Tabitha Twitchit reverses hastily into the shelter afforded by the branches of the nearest tree.

The gardens are a delight for both cats: informal in nature, and with great variety of planting, they allow the cats to display a more gregarious side to their nature, accompanying visitors as they wander through. Both cats like the Great Pond, created by the monks as a fish pond, and spend hours watching the water as it courses down from the Great Pond along a canal that connects the Mermaid and Long Ponds. Fruitless fishing could be the official name of the activity here: cats can do many things, but watching these two splashing at the sight of a fish is hilarious. As is their reaction to frogs: both cats sit still for hours, ears forward, noses almost touching a large frog, until it moves, at which point the cats leap into the air in fright. It doesn't matter how many times they do it, the outcome is always the same.

All this outdoor activity, however, is a only a way of filling the time until the house settles down, the grandchildren go, and dogs fall asleep. Then both Tabitha Twitchit and Tilly return to take their rightful place in the Abbey.

OPENING PAGE
Tabitha Twitchit: looking for cook
LEFT
Tilly likes to keep her distance
RIGHT
Tilly prefers scaling walls to being in the cloister

Marmion and Hildegard
Order of St Benedict, Glenstal Abbey

'When all, therefore, are gathered together, let them say Compline; and when they come out from Compline, no one shall be allowed to say anything from that time on.'

From the Rule of St Benedict

Ireland is not a country with much of a 'cat' tradition, so to find a Benedictine monastery that has cats is something of a curiosity. It happened, it seems, almost by accident: there was a local custom of dumping unwanted pets in the monastery grounds, and the monks put great effort into re-homing these discarded animals. Two cats, a jovial tabby with a white chin and a stocky black and white bi-colour, stayed put. They were named Marmion and Hildegard. Opinion was divided among the community about cats: some didn't like or want them, others were keen to have a cat or two.

My interest in the two cats at Glenstal was certainly a matter of some amusement among the community.

HISTORY

Glenstal Abbey is an imposing Norman Revivalist castle, with the round-tower style of Windsor Castle, and surrounded by extensive woodlands. The original castle is now occupied by the school while the monastery itself is housed in newer buildings with their own internal courtyard. Built as a family seat in the early 19th century, but abandoned in the Irish Civil War, the castle was eventually offered as a religious house, with the aim of establishing the first major Benedictine presence in Ireland since the Henrician and Elizabethan confiscations of four hundred years before.

After a warm welcome from Prior Dominic, I explained what I was doing, and what I needed to accomplish during my visit; he arranged for me to meet some of the monks who had contact with Marmion and Hildegard. Something told me that he was wondering why on earth someone should want to produce a book about cats, least of all cats in cloistered communities He warned me that it might be difficult to find them, and that even when found, they would be unlikely to be cooperative.

The cats are based comfortably in two 'kennels' adjacent to the new monastic buildings. Their official purpose is rodent control. Their unstated purpose is subtler, one only a cat-lover could understand; the gift of feline grace, of companionship without obligation.

There are those who just tolerate their presence, and there are others who actively welcome them, among them the kitchener, Father Anslem, who ensures that Marmion and Hildegard are amply fed. Father Brian, whose green fingers and plant expertise are evident throughout the gardens, is also sanguine about the cats. I also sensed that a number of monks – though they might not publicly avow it – found in the cats a leavening quality. Father Mark, the Abbey historian, was also unperturbed by the idea of cats at the Abbey, while Father Simon remarked to me with a grin that 'Cats remind monks not to be catty'.

As with all who follow the Rule of St Benedict, there are rules. The most important rule that the cats have to follow is 'No howling during the night silence'. How this is enforced I can't imagine, but I am told that the cats abide by it. It may be that when either Marmion or Hildegard get the urge for a nocturnal howl, they seek out a far off 'howling corner' somewhere on the estate of some 500 acres! The other simple, and self-imposed, rule that the cats follow is that they stay enclosed within the monastery and its grounds, having no contact with the school.

All I can say is that the Prior's warning that the cats might not show up proved groundless: I went into the enclosed garden, and within minutes both Hildegard and Marmion were winding round my ankles, in that perverse way that cats have, of doing exactly the opposite of what is expected. While taking photos, I did notice a group of monks observing us through the windows, some at least presumably wondering what on earth possessed this mad Englishman to be bothering with their cats.

OPENING PAGE
Marmion is a real guardian cat
LEFT
Hildegard and Marmion were surprisingly cooperative
BELOW
Hildegard wonders whether there might be another snack

Jane
St Monica's Priory, Hoxton

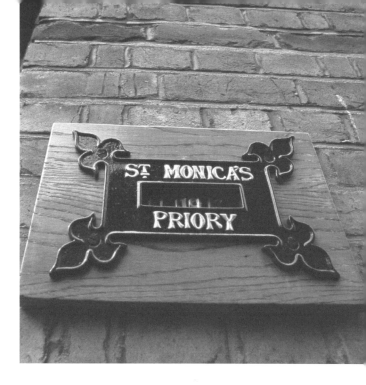

'Those in charge of the pantry, or of clothing and books, should render cheerful service to their brothers.'

From the Rule of St Augustine

Jane is a portly black cat with startling yellow eyes, who lives with the Augustinian friars of St Monica's Priory in East London's Hoxton. She arrived as a gift from the architect who was working on the parish church adjacent to this modest little priory. The August-inians differ from monastic orders, in that there has always been emphasis on the friars serving in parishes, rather than living apart. So although at first St Monica's appears to be in an unlikely setting for a priory, it actually exemplifies the mendicant Augustinian principle – and as such, Jane (the cat) is considered a part of the community, not one priest's pet.

The friars, Father Mark and Father Paul, divide their time between supporting the needy, attending to the

HISTORY

This diminutive priory is no more than a soot-stained brick Victorian house adjacent to a parish church, its appearance a throwback to the days when Hoxton was ''oxton', an area of pie and mash stalls, apprehensive London cab drivers, and the kind of characters who populate gangster movies. Heavily gentrified now, the 'Hoxton Mission' as it was originally envisaged still does important work in this community.

everyday needs of the parish, supporting the chaplaincy at London University, and celebrating masses at a nearby prison, as well as their own spiritual practice. The priory serves a multi-cultural community (the Christmas blessing is given in twenty different languages), and it is the first Augustinian Priory to be founded since the Reformation.

As a terrified kitten, Jane seldom ventured out of the basement, emerging apprehensively from time to time to greet Father Paul or Father Mark as they went about their daily routine in the Priory. With patience and care, she was encouraged to come out and up into the main house, and eventually plucked up enough courage to follow the friars into the main church for evening prayers. Soon she was investigating the rest of the Priory house, and making cautious sorties outside. Here she sharpened her urban street skills, learning to dodge suicidal motor cycle couriers, rage-filled cyclists and insane white van drivers. Her explorations took her around the newly-opened fashionable bars and galleries that line Hoxton Square; but when she realized that it was easier to get a lychee martini than a drink of milk, Jane decided that being streetwise, in her case, meant deciding to mainly stay put inside the priory. The bizarre fashionable goings-on in the square were as easily, and more safely, observed from Father Mark's bedroom window.

So, having turned her back on the frenetic world of BritArt celebrities and the trendy gangster chic of London's East End, Jane moved on to explore the world at the back of the Priory, a maze of gloomy brick walled alleyways reminiscent of Jack the Ripper. The spot she adopted was an almost subterranean alley separating the Priory house from the parish school: a tangle of overgrown grass and self-seeded lilac bushes, it seemed to offer a perfect and private outdoor haven for Jane. But this peaceful setting turned out to be illusory: a startled Jane discovered that young children throw balls with more enthusiasm than judgement, and retreated in haste from the hail of mis-thrown tennis balls that cascaded over the wall during outdoor physical education classes.

So Jane returned to the safety of the priory and parish church; but changes were afoot here too. Long-awaited work to convert the basement into a parish room was beginning, entailing noisy excavation work, and the loss of her sleeping quarters (Jane had previously divided her nights between her basket and a much more secluded coal bunker). At the same time a road crew arrived to start digging up the pavement outside the Priory. Assailed by noise on all sides, Jane looked to a higher place in search of peace and quiet. She decided to join Father Mark in his room, away from the racket of machinery, where she watched with interest as he spent hours at his desk, sorting out various selections of beads for the rosaries that he was making. She even tried to get involved in the process too, batting beads from one pile to another, sending them skittering across the desk. It took Father Mark a while to work out why he was assembling such mismatched sets of rosary beads, and Jane was informed that her assistance, while welcome in principle, was in fact not that helpful. She didn't take much notice, as is the way with cats, continuing to surreptitiously roll beads from one sorted group to another when Father Mark was away from his desk. Any exclamation of exasperation at this continued attempt to involve herself in this cottage industry activity is greeted by a look of startled amazement on Jane's part. She just walks to the door, looking over her shoulder as if to say 'How could you think such a thing of me? I was merely looking out of the window.'

OPENING PAGE
Jane prefers to sleep in the coal bunker
BELOW
Looking for peace and quiet

Splash
The Iona Community, Iona Abbey

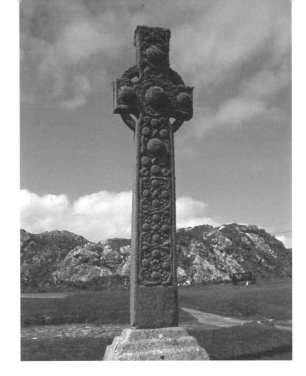

In Praise of Colum Cille
'It was not on cushioned beds
he bent to his complex prayers:
he crucified – not for crimes –
his body on the grey waves.
He stakes the marvellous claim
when Mo Chummae set down in Iona.
It's more than anyone can grasp,
what the King did for his sake.'

Attributed to Beccan mac Luigdech, c.630

This tiny island off the western tip of the Isle of Mull in the west of Scotland is an inspiration for many. The Iona Community is a grouping of people committed to Christian values who are spread throughout the world, dedicated to social justice, peace and ecumenism through their Christian life. On their behalf, the staff based on the island run the Abbey, and its sister the MacLeod Centre, as residential centres, and maintain daily worship in the Abbey Church. One such is Catherine, a Canadian member of staff who

HISTORY

From the mainland, Iona seems to be suspended on the edge of the physical world. For 1500 years it has been a place of pilgrimage, and the burial place of kings. St Columba and his followers landed here from Ireland, and built the first monastery, a crude settlement of clay and wattle buildings. The present Abbey building was constructed by the Benedictines in the 13th century. The 8th Duke of Argyll initiated the restoration of the Abbey Church and today the Abbey fabric is maintained by Historic Scotland. Founded by the Reverend George MacLeod in the 1930s, the Iona Community grew up around the rebuilding of the remaining monastic buildings.

exploring the intricate stonework of the Abbey, and was walking through the cloisters in the gathering dusk. She recalls an uncanny sensation of being watched, and glancing up into the cloister rafters, she saw a face peering out of the near darkness at her. But this was no imp, nor an animated gargoyle. Its eyes blinked, Catherine stopped, and Splash hopped down from the cloister ceiling to bid her first greeting to the person who would become one of her principal carers.

Splash had originally come to the island with a young staff member; she had not been happy in the city, and seeing the gusto with which she greeted the freedom of island life, it was decided that Splash should stay even when her owner left. She is deaf, and life on an island with a minimum of road traffic was as safe as it could get for her. I'm sure that Splash missed her original owner at some point, but she was having too much fun exploring this extraordinary new environment to bid a fond farewell. First of all, there were winding trails through peat bogs and hillocks to explore. Who cared if Splash couldn't hear the outraged shrieks of nesting seabirds? Splash didn't: the first thing she knew about it was when she was dive bombed by a furious seagull. Having been brought up in the city, Splash knew all about unidentified flying objects, so wasn't much bothered.

There are pristine beaches of white sand nearby, from which Splash can watch eider ducks bobbing up and down on the waves. Then there are visitors to

has been on the island for three years. Her family was a real 'cat' family, and such is her regard for cats that she told me she would not have come to Iona if it had meant leaving all cats behind.

Catherine's first meeting with Splash, the Iona Abbey cat, was unusual. She had spent an afternoon accompany: during the summer, a never-ending stream of them, and Splash often walks down to the ruined nunnery, where she sits on the wall, watching for passers-by.

Splash has one odd habit: she talks constantly to herself. So, when there's music in the Abbey, Splash will often come in. Maybe she detects the music through airborne vibrations, but invariably she joins in, adding her cat crooning to the voices of the assembled worshippers in a valiant, but horribly discordant, attempt to sing counterpart. Her startling vocalism is used to better effect in Dunsmeorach, the nearby house for resident staff. Whereas a hearing cat would sit outside someone's door, meowing to be let in, Splash simply yowls and growls discordantly in the hallway, until everyone opens his or her doors. Three of the resident staff have been yowled into submission, and sleep with their doors left open, in order to get an uninterrupted night's sleep.

She also talks to herself when she's wandering around through the nearby graves, or walking the paths that connect the various community houses. I'd love to know what she's saying. I suspect it is something along the lines of 'what's for supper', or 'must duff up Tiger (an intruder Abbey cat) next time I see him'. Anyway, whatever her thoughts are, there's no doubt that life on this magical island in the care of the Iona Community is the best thing that has ever happened to her.

OPENING PAGE
Splash constantly talks to herself
LEFT
Waiting to waylay Abbey visitors
RIGHT
In the safety of Dunsmeorach

Oliver
Convent of the Poor Clares, Lynton

'Let the sisters to whom the Lord has given the grace of working, work faithfully and devotedly after the Hour of Terce at work that pertains to a virtuous life and the common good.'

From the Rule of St Clare

The only member of the community not bound by a vow of obedience is Oliver, who is certainly one of the little treasures of the Poor Clare Convent in Lynton, on the North Devon Coast. A chunky black cat with a proprietorial air, he's watched over by bright-eyed and weather-beaten Sister Mary Magdalen, who seems to know his every habit and move.

Oliver is the latest of a succession of cats at the convent that started when a ginger cat, Marguerita, moved into the convent grounds to have her kittens. As opinion among the sisters was divided as to the joys of having a resident cat, Marguerita was cared for outside in an outbuilding; she laid a long and fruitless siege to the convent buildings. Then came Tom, a total

HISTORY

This small enclosed community, fronting onto Lynton's main street, has been here since 1911, leading a life of prayer and reflection, supporting themselves by sales of home-made jam (the cloisters are stacked with piles of cheerfully capped jars), the manufacture of small gifts, and the retailing of altar breads. Even at the height of the summer tourist season, there is an air of peace and calm.

and unapproachable stray, who kept himself warm on the ashes of bonfires in the convent grounds. This dishevelled and wild fellow succeeded in overturning the (contested) rule forbidding resident cats inside the convent buildings. Sister Mary Magdalen had been gradually getting Tom to allow her closer and closer, eventually persuading him to settle in the greenhouse. One day he appeared with a badly infected eye: the RSPCA was contacted, and on being told Tom was a 'bit' wild, turned up with apparatus more appropriate for catching a tiger than a cat! To everyone's amazement Tom, confronted by a pole with a loop on the end, clambered meekly into the container prepared for him, and was carted away.

Sister Mary Magdalen was convinced that he'd be put down, but a few days later, the RSPCA brought him back, minus one eye, all spruced up, inoculated and in surprisingly good shape. The vet had been so impressed by Tom's spirit that he had been given a special 'hospital' name – Captain. But, unbelievably, disaster struck Tom again: he developed a serious infection in his other eye, which had to be removed in a second traumatic operation. The sisters wondered if he would survive and how they could care for a blind cat; if prayers are answered by a miracle, theirs certainly were: Tom came back a changed character; friendly and trusting of all the sisters, he faultlessly navigated his way around the convent. Watching him,

it was impossible to tell that he was blind. Staircases, corners, furniture; nothing presented an obstacle.

After Tom, came Mogs. She was brought by the family of one of the sisters, who had been picnicking on Exmoor, on their way to Lynton. In the middle of their picnic, a bedraggled soaking cat sprang into the back of their car and refused to get out. After wolfing down all the remaining chicken soup, she was brought to the convent and given shelter. If there was ever a cat to convince doubters of how domestic a cat could be, it was Mogs: she used the WC then called for it to be flushed, and to elicit sympathy she'd fake a limp, hobbling along in front of a sister, only reverting to a sprightly trot when she thought she was no longer being observed.

The next cat was YoYo, who came from the RSPCA, who were by now in awe of the sisters' astonishing ability to turn hopeless cases into real successes. YoYo had originally been called Joseph, but Sister Joseph did not want to be confused with a cat, so a Swedish sister, who'd always struggled with her 'J' sounds, named him JoJo – but since it always came out as 'YoYo', 'YoYo' he became.

By now cats had become an established feature of the convent, and after YoYo passed away, the sisters contacted the Barnstaple RSPCA. They did have two brother cats that needed re-homing, ominously named Reggie and Ronnie, after the notorious East End crime bosses, Reggie and Ronnie Kray. Ronnie proved too wild to be re-housed, but Reggie seemed to be looking for salvation, and was brought to the convent, and renamed Oliver. He took to convent life as if made for it. Those who permit it receive regular visits from Oliver to their rooms. He uses the refectory window as his 'cat flap', and guards the bread cupboard from unwanted rodent raiders. Oliver has recently got 'religion' in a big way.

Murphy
Mottisfont Abbey

'They are to be given all that their health requires even if, during their time in the world, poverty made it impossible for them to find the very necessities of life.'

From the Purpose and Basis for Common Life,

The Rule of St Augustine

It is remarkable how many of the original signs of Mottisfont's origins as a monastery remain discernable. The original Priory was reputed to be a place of pilgrimage and miracles, owing to the presence of one of the fingers of St John the Baptist (who presumably had forty fingers on each hand, judging by the number of medieval shrines claiming possession of a digit). Although its demise as a priory was due to the dissolution of monasteries in the time of Henry VIII, the number of canons had already diminished, due to the Black Death, to an unsustainable three. Much of the Tudor renovation work was replaced during the 18th century, by Sir Richard Mill's extensive alterations; yet the monastic remains were carefully preserved during this time.

HISTORY

For those who are aware of them, Mottisfont's monastic origins are easy to discern. The church, the remains of the cloisters, and the vaulted undercroft all bear witness to the lives of the Augustinian friars during the Middle Ages, which were carefully preserved when Sir Richard Mills' alterations replaced earlier Tudor renovations. The beautiful gardens and National Collection of old-fashioned roses are now at the heart of its appeal and it belongs to the National Trust.

Only at around this time did the priory become known as Mottisfont Abbey.

Among the many pleasures of Mottisfont are the gardens. Wide expanses of lawn are interspersed with woodland; the walled garden holds a treasure trove of herbaceous plants, and hosts the National Collection of old-fashioned roses. At the bottom of the gardens, the River Test flows gently through the grounds, exiting noisily through the remains of an old millrace; and this is where the visitor is most likely to meet Murphy, the Mottisfont Abbey cat. There's a bridge spanning the river, just upstream from the old mill race: as any angler will know, the River Test is a prime trout stream, and although Murphy will never know the pleasures of fly-fishing, he certainly knows those of trout watching, and at moments he has been within a whisker of diving headlong into the river. Murphy may also be found sheltering from the rain in the ticket office, from where he cheerfully accompanies visitors along the river to the thatched fishing hut.

Murphy's predecessor, Jimmy, had lived in the potting sheds, and his job was to deter rabbits from chewing the rose shoots. When Murphy arrived from the aptly named Nine Lives Animal Shelter, the transition from his former life – as a maltreated cat from a drug-addict household who wound up dumped in a dustbin – was almost more than he could cope with. He was settled into the potting sheds, where he stayed for a few weeks, and emerged only to disappear for five or six

weeks. He was found about four miles away, and duly brought back. After a few more weeks of being cared for in the potting sheds (where David Stone prefers him to be), he emerged a transformed cat.

Murphy is a cat with a number of routines. The gardeners' mess is his daytime base; here he is fed, by one of the gardeners, Matt Wavell. From the mess Murphy sallies forth, wanders down to the house; here he sits, eyeing a large magnolia that grows up to the top of the house. Then he hauls himself painstakingly up, teetering along branches that can hardly support the weight of a mouse, let alone a cat. Once at the top, he starts down again. This is heart stopping for the observer, as he has to lower himself rear end first. More than one passer by has been startled by a scrabbling and crashing noise as Murphy tumbles down, emerging on the ground with a half-annoyed, half-embarrassed look on his face. It doesn't deter him from climbing other trees, either. He was once sitting concealed in a laurel tree that was being pruned;

unfortunately the branch being pruned was the one he was lying on. He also regularly scrambles up the enormous London Plane that grows near the river, yet he still hasn't learnt that it's easier to climb up than to get down. So the garden echoes to the crashes of Murphy tumbling out of various trees, like a furry conker. But perhaps the best time to see Murphy in action is during the autumn, when he is engaged in everlasting pursuit of wind-blown leaves.

Murphy likes to visit the house, where he lies stretched out on a leather settee, greeting visitors. If he takes a liking to a particular visitor, he may well go on the house tour as well. Murphy also has a keen interest in the special events that take place in the grounds from time to time: he recently took part – inadvertently – in an open-air performance of Wind in the Willows, before deciding that human-sized rats, moles and badgers, combined with a gigantic toad and various weasels, were really not his dish of milk.

OPENING PAGE
A familiar sight for Abbey visitors
LEFT
Murphy watches out for Matt and David
RIGHT
On his garden rounds

Oscar
The Society of All Saints Sisters of the Poor, All Saints Convent, Oxford

'Although human nature itself is drawn to special kindness towards the old and children, still the Rule should also provide for them.'

On children and the old, from the Rule of St Benedict

Oscar is a languid and slightly foppish tiger tabby, given to bursts of kitten-like play when he thinks no one is looking. His introduction to All Saints was through Sandra George, PA to the head of St John's (the home for the elderly). Noticing that some of the residents missed their former pets, she argued the case for having an animal – preferably a cat. The cat she needed would have to be confident, and totally at ease with people. He'd also have to cope with a dog called Oscar. A call came from a local animal rescue centre that they had a suitable cat: he'd been left behind when his owners moved.

'Did the cat have a name', she enquired? 'Yes', came the answer: 'Oscar'.

HISTORY
The Convent of All Saints is part of an extensive and bustling complex that includes a home for the elderly, hospices for both children and 16-40 year olds, and a drop-in centre for the homeless. The nuns engage in pastoral visiting, preaching and public speaking, hospitality and spiritual direction alongside their responsibilities for these services. The order was founded in 1851 as a nursing order, part of the Anglican 're-invention' of monastic life. Many of the Sisters distinguished themselves by working alongside the newly-formed Red Cross in the Franco-Prussian war.

Oscar the cat was adopted with delight by some of the elderly residents: one in particular, Evelyn, will vacate her bed to make sure that Oscar has a warm spot on which to sleep. And as well as making himself at home in the residential home area of St. John's, Oscar made himself at home in the convent too. A little too much at home sometimes: Sister Mary Julian, who had been given the brief of ensuring that Oscar behaved in the private areas of the house, had kept quiet about Oscar's habit of secreting himself under the altar. But his chapel-going habits were not always circumspect: being a cat that relishes extreme warmth, he liked to sit near clusters of lit candles. A cat sitting in candlelight is not exactly well concealed, and so it was that Oscar was gently chided, and banned from the chapel. Now he just waits outside, and when the nuns exit from a solemn eucharist, Oscar hurtles to the head of the queue for the ensuing coffee and biscuits.

So Oscar met Oscar. The two animals coped only by studiously ignoring each other. Oscar (canine) liked cats, and would play endlessly with them outside in the grounds. But visiting cats were unsure about this, as they found it hard to tell the difference between a playful Oscar the dog, and a potentially life-threatening canine monster. There was some initial confusion: both Oscars turned up expectantly at each other's feeding times. But no matter how hard Oscar the dog tried to make friends with his new feline namesake, Oscar (feline) wouldn't have any of it, so in the end they simply settled for ignoring each other.

He has developed an appetite for the morning papers too: they are put on a table in the panelled entrance hall, and Oscar waits impatiently for their delivery. No one else gets a look in until well into the afternoon, as Oscar lies on top of the pile, an absolute deadweight that simply slithers through one's hands if one tries to move him. He likes diaries too, and slumps lazily across the current day's page, as if to say, 'I am today's most important event'.

Oscar is a cat with a schedule: he has Sunday breakfast with the deputy head of the residential care home; he waits to join the sisters at the end of their offices; he visits the residents in the care home. He was recently diagnosed with hyperthyroidism, and although he's responding well to treatment, has started to exploit the fact that people think he's unwell. When Oscar is outside, and no one is looking, he plays animated games of chase with wind-blown leaves; once inside, he affects extreme fatigue, taking the lift up to the first floor, and generally appearing weary and worn-out. His friend Evelyn – the lady who always gives Oscar the warm spot on her bed – has an electric wheelchair.

Oscar often hitches a ride with her, and to the delight of all the residents takes a tour of the residential unit, sitting on Evelyn's lap. He smiles regally at everyone as he passes, a posture that is slightly spoilt by the fact that Evelyn isn't the best driver in the world. But Oscar braces himself, gets a firm grip on the blanket, and takes the abrupt starts and stops, occasional bumps and jerky reversing in his stride, as he and a beaming Evelyn whirr their way along the corridors of the residential unit.

OPENING PAGE
Oscar, gently chided, and banned from the chapel

LEFT
No one gets the papers until Oscar has finished with them

RIGHT
A cat who plays like a kitten when no one is looking

Neri and Fiona
Holy Hill Hermitage, Skreen, Co. Sligo

'If the prior and brothers see fit, you may have foundations in solitary places, or where you are given a site that is suitable and convenient for the observance proper to your Order.'

From the Carmelite Rule of St Albert

When they first came here, the community inherited an old sheep dog from the Sisters of Mercy who had previously occupied the manor house. As one of the stated aims of the community is to be close to nature, it was only natural that cats would be welcomed too. A Sligo vet asked whether they might like two cats in his care – Fiona, a part-tortoiseshell, and Iona. Fiona was half-wild, and initially struggled with the concept of community life, disappearing for weeks on end. Neri, a bicolour black and white cat with a striking aquiline profile, came from the litter of a feral cat, Bridie, who had adopted Father John, and ended up giving birth on Father John's lap, to a litter of six kittens. Neri was initially traumatized by other feral cats, and embraced the concept of solitary living by spending his early

HISTORY

In 1995, monks from the Spiritual Life Institute in the USA and Canada were invited by an Irish bishop to create a hermitage in northwest Ireland. The 200-year-old manor house and convent being offered was in complete contrast to their previous hermitages in Nova Scotia and Arizona, but its dilapidated condition made for months of hard work to renovate the buildings, and install a library and chapel as well as separate hermitages in the grounds. The result, however, has an organic feel that ensures it fits well within the landscape and offers a real escape from the bustle of the modern world.

days under a blanket. This led to surprise encounters for those who inadvertently sat on him. It is still advisable to check under a blanket before sitting down.

The principal building of the new hermitage centre was a dilapidated manor house, surrounded by its derelict outbuildings. With local help, the monks re-roofed it, replaced windows, repaired and restored the outbuildings, and built two new 'cottage' hermitages in the extensive grounds. They installed a restful library and chapel in the top of the manor house, and established several sitting rooms for guests on the ground floor; they have also created exquisite garden areas within the grounds. The result is an inspiring

meeting of the wild and the cultivated – wild meadow, islands of floral and foliage colour, bordered by a small river that flows down from the Ox mountains. There has never been a 'master plan' for Holy Hill, and as such it has an organic feel, as if the diminutive stone cottages dotting the grounds have simply grown rather than being constructed.

Of the two cats, Fiona is the shyer. She studiously ignores the two community dogs – Duende, a lumbering and companionable Newfoundland, and Sedona, a rescue spaniel – whereas Neri takes every opportunity to tease them. The poor dogs do their best to ignore Neri, but sooner or later he succeeds in

provoking indignant barking. And although Neri may derive a lot of pleasure from dog teasing, he seems to have learnt from them too: he defended the newly planted lawns from the attention of wandering sheep, and it was quite a sight to see seven or eight sheep fleeing over neighbouring fields, with Neri in hot pursuit. He also plays with and chases marauding foxes, a more risky and serious business. Fiona is warier: leaving the drama to Neri, she contents herself with the occasional attack on a wind-tossed daffodil – an encounter where the daffodil is as likely as her to be the victor. She's also quite a soccer cat too, and spends hours swiping a ball of paper into an improvised goal, such as an overturned wastepaper basket.

OPENING PAGE

Neri in the spring garden

LEFT

Fiona: a feline soccer star

RIGHT

Neri's aristocratic profile

Both cats revel in the garden; monks and visitors are regularly greeted by one or other of the cats hopping out of the undergrowth, to join them as they walk through the grounds. Neri and Fiona are always on hand when there's work going on outside. Digging excites them, as does weeding in the vegetable patch. Their techniques aren't too good: what they most like doing is flopping down in the exact place where you want to dig, and scuffing through a pile of weeds, spreading it out so that it can be gathered up again. Life at Holy Hill is marked by periods of silence for community and visitors alike. And solitude can be hard work. So the cats introduce an element of unobtrusive and undemanding company, punctuated by interruptions that serve to remind those who contemplate in solitude that, at Holy Hill, the community places great value on staying close to nature.

RIGHT
Fiona joins visitors for a garden walk
FAR RIGHT
Indulging in some wood-carving

Smudge
The Order of Buddhist Contemplatives, Throssel Hole Buddhist Abbey

'Do good for others. To cease from evil is to devote one's life to the good of all living things.'

From the Three Pure Buddhist Precepts

A reverence for all forms of life is perhaps the best-known feature of Buddhist teaching, and at Throssel Hole Buddhist Abbey, amid the remote and austere beauty of the Northumberland moors, a moss carpeted corner – protected by a dry stone wall and overhanging rowan trees – is the setting for a touching animal graveyard, whose simple stones mark the burial places of many loved animals.

Visitors arriving at the abbey are more than likely to be greeted by Smudge, a black and white cat with the distinctive facial markings of a cat from a Japanese print. Smudge is officially the novices' cat. He was introduced to the monastery by the Abbot, as a replacement for Jane, the former novices' cat, who had

HISTORY

This remote community was founded by the Reverend Master Jiyu-Kennett in 1972, following the Soto Zen tradition. The early days of the community were tough, to say the least. While the monks worked on rebuilding the original farmhouse, meditation took place in a draughty old barn, with snow blowing in through cracks in the doors and windows. As the community grew, the monks developed and adapted the farm buildings to cope with the demands of a growing community and congregation.

died at the venerable age of twenty. The Abbot had found him at a Cat Rescue Centre in Newcastle. The contrast of his early life of abandonment with the serene monastic life of Throssel Hole had little effect on this ebullient kitten. Smudge does not have the quiet reverent demeanour of the monks: he lolls about in the novices' common room, hogging the radiator, wanders the abbey as if he owns it, and on Sunday evenings, when the television is turned on, he takes the best spot. In a tidy monastery, the tell tale signs of Smudge's passing are the screwed up paper balls that he uses to play soccer with the monks.

The Prior, Reverend Alicia, told me that Smudge is an eager and sometimes distracting participant in the day-to-day devotions of the monks. One of Smudge's constant ambitions is to get into the Meditation Hall. During the summer, when the doors are left open to allow cool air to circulate, access is easy. If Smudge had any sense at all, he'd slink in, keep a low profile, and try to blend in with the crowd; but Smudge is so pleased to get in that he just has to say 'hello' to everybody. In the winter, getting into the Meditation Hall isn't so easy, as the doors are kept closed. His trick here is to lie in wait for the Abbot to process out: Smudge dashes in around the Abbot's feet before anyone can stop him. He likes the Meditation Hall, because it's where the monks are. However, his habit of butting against a monk who is practising meditation is definitely considered too distracting, and he is forever being gently but firmly deposited outside. It's a game to Smudge, and one he'll never stop trying to win.

Smudge has a whole panoply of methods by which he tries to draw attention to himself. Outdoors he will lurk in a bush, with one foreleg extended into the open, trying to snag the leg of an unwary passer by. Indoors Smudge has his work cut out to catch the attention of a passing monk. He'll sit in strategic parts of the monastery, waiting for someone to come along. When someone does approach him, he straightens up, looking smart and alert. Most times he'll get a friendly greeting, but cats can be so demanding. So if that isn't enough and Smudge can't get the attention he wants, he'll take himself off to find the monk specially assigned to his care, and make himself a nuisance there.

OPENING PAGE
The Meditation Hall is a favourite
spot for Smudge
LEFT
Officially, Smudge is the novices' cat
RIGHT
A moment of contemplation

Mellagel, Miri and Merlin

The Society of the Sacred Cross, The Tymawr Community

'Therefore let the Abbess show equal love to all, and impose the same discipline on all, according to their deserts.'

From the Rule of Saint Benedict on the requisite qualities of an Abbess

The grand old cat of Tymawr is Merlin, whose magical namesake might easily have orchestrated my arrival at the convent. Driving in a torrential downpour down a winding lane – overshadowed on either side by deformed moss-covered trees – I came to a sharp bend flooded by an overflowing river. Lying across the lane was a fallen tree, with a disconsolate looking sister on the other side, sitting in her car. After considerable effort (and some unmonastic sotto voce murmurings on my part), the tree was dragged aside enough to permit one car at a time to pass. The sister thanked

HISTORY

The small community of Tymawr lies deep in the wooded valleys of Monmouthshire, on the Welsh borders. A community of ten nuns lives here, dedicating much of the day to silent prayer, interspersed with work and recreation in the house and grounds. The community was founded in 1924, from a Society founded in Chichester in 1914, whose purpose was to encourage a disciplined life of study and prayer. Tymawr became a recognised contemplative community in the 1930s, and is supported by a network of oblates and associates, as well as the activities of a retreat house in the grounds, and conferences.

me, and as she drove off, her car's silencer fell off, streaming sparks as it scraped along the metalled road. Another halt, and after several failed attempts at a temporary repair, we processed slowly back to the convent.

Sister Laurie was waiting there, sheltering from the rain, and with her two of the most impish young cats I have met – Miri, a Siamese cross of nine months, and Mellagel, an eight month old ginger-and-white cat. Miri is Welsh for gaiety, and Mellagel for merriment. It would be hard to find two more irrepressible and

mischievous cats: impervious to the rain (and there's a lot of it here), the two cats were busy poking their heads into pots, clawing up the wooden uprights of the porch, and generally doing things that a right-minded cat would certainly reserve for better weather.

Merlin, it was explained to me, lived in secluded retirement. In his prime he had been a true woodsman, it seemed, and the close companion of another community cat, Bronwyn. Bronwyn had lived at Tymawr for twenty-four years, and was joined by

Merlin when she was twelve: the two cats had struck up a close friendship, curling up to sleep each night in a specially provided crib set at the back of the convent chapel. After Bronwyn's death, Merlin retired. He relinquished his role as a woodsman cat and when Mellagel and Miri came, he threw up his paws in disgust, retreating to the calm of a sitting-room in the top of the convent. I saw Merlin in his lofty lair – he cocked one eye at me as if to say 'Nearly got you, didn't I', before going resolutely back to sleep again.

The two kittens had regarded Merlin as a larger version of themselves, always there to be pounced upon, teased and dashed at. Mellagel in particular, having come from a barn cat litter, was perhaps a little rougher than she might have been. She can certainly hold her own, even at only eight months old, with any visiting dog. The last dog to visit spent the entire time sitting anxiously in his owner's car wondering exactly what he'd done wrong, as Mellagel growled and hissed through the windscreen at him.

So Merlin's peace had to be secured by providing the two kittens with a small 'house', under the shelter of a long covered verandah. Their view from here gives them a perfect chance to review all who come up the drive (especially those foolish enough to come with dogs). As the community ran a working dairy farm until the mid-1980s, there are a number of barns and sheds for the cats to explore. The sisters have also undertaken a great deal of conservation work, planting a small wood, and recovering and restoring the Victorian Fish Pond. Miri and Mellagel frequently visit the pond, indulging in fruitless splashy attempts to catch the fish therein. They watch in open-mouthed amazement as the sisters work from a canoe to clear debris and weeds. All this watery activity must explain their easy attitude to getting wet. My last sight of the two cats was of Mellagel smacking her paw into a puddle, whilst Miri stood (rather foolishly in my opinion) gawping at the puddle, trying to work out where the sudden shower of water drops was coming from. There is a lot of rain in Monmouthshire, after all, so two water-resistant cats are a perfect complement.

LEFT
Plotting mischief
BELOW
A rare moment of inactivity

Bonnie
The Society of St Margaret, Walsingham Priory

'We see in these swift and skilful travellers a symbol of our life, which seeks to be a pilgrimage and a passage on this earth for the way of heaven.'

Pope Paul VI

Bonnie, the Walsingham Priory cat, has not always been in the religious life. She is in the care of Sister Jane Louise, whose cat she has been for 16 years. Some time before joining the order, Sister Jane Louise had moved to Cornwall, leaving her then cat in the care of a trusted friend. Once she'd settled in to her new surroundings, Sister Jane Louise enquired as to how her cat had settled in its new home back in London. 'Fine', came the reply; in fact so well that it would have been unkind to uproot her. Jane Louise felt the absence of her cat keenly, and by accident rather than design, found a companion in the form of a tiny Cornish village kitten, whom she called Bonnie. Then, acquiescing to her vocation, Jane Louise applied to join the Society of St Margaret at Walsingham, and was

HISTORY

The Society of St Margaret at Walsingham is one of a number of religious groups represented at Walsingham, the site of one of Europe's great shrines. The priory is adjacent to the Anglican shrine, and is home to a community of some twelve sisters. The priory was founded in the 1950s by some of the society's sisters from Haggerston, in response to the revitalisation of interest in pilgrimages, and the main work of the Priory lies in giving hospitality for pilgrims, and educational and pastoral work.

warmly welcomed at the Priory, and as Jane Louise settled into her novitiate, so Bonnie settled into hers. Bonnie's introductory time had its complications. Not with Katie the dog: Bonnie had made friends with Katie the moment she had been let out of her basket. They'd touched noses, and agreed to follow monastic principles of peaceful co-existence.

No, the aforementioned complications centred around the very odd welcome she got from Garfield, who was waiting for her in the inner courtyard garden: he started to walk around her in circles. 'This must be what you do,' thought Bonnie after a while, and she started to walk around Garfield in circles. Now, it's very confusing when two cats try to walk around each other in circles. The two cats made a pattern a bit like that of the earth and the moon in opposing orbits. If you can imagine Bonnie at the centre, with Garfield describing a large circle around her, and then imagine Garfield, circling around where Bonnie had been, but Bonnie wasn't there any more, she was now describing a tighter circle around Garfield, then… As I said, it was confusing.

The two cats intermittently continued this highly eccentric orbital dance for weeks. There was no overt aggression, just the chaotic dance. The sisters were beginning to suffer giddiness from watching this endless movement, Katie had retired with a headache, and Sister Jane Louise decided that enough was enough: the two cats must surely have got used to each

accepted. 'Would it be a problem', she enquired, 'if my cat Bonnie came too?' The answer was encouraging: she'd be welcome to bring her cat, to join the dog and cat already in residence.

So Jane Louise and Bonnie set off on the long journey from Cornwall to Norfolk. Not without event, as Bonnie nearly escaped twice on the way. She was other by now, even if only in passing (as it were), and put Bonnie in her room, with firm instructions to only walk in straight lines henceforth. A period of separation enabled a more normal spatial relationship to be established between the two cats, and life settled into its natural rhythm. Bonnie explored the nearby shrine, wandering around, greeting the odd pilgrim or two, and stood outside the shrine refectory trying (unsuccessfully) to look abandoned and unfed.

With the passing of years, Bonnie's attention has gradually turned to the inner life of the Priory: she has started to creep into the chapel while the sisters are at prayer, giving an affectionate head butt to those who seemed not to notice her, hopping onto the altar to sniff the flowers. She'll sit for hours, as still as a statue, in the arched windows that overlook the sanctuary, watching the various services and offices. She has developed some more cranky habits too, like that of nipping the toes of sisters who wear open sandals: it says a lot for the sisters of the Society of St Margaret that they just smile kindly, and resist the impulse to let those sandalled feet just let slip a gentle prod.

Billy Boy, Ozzie and Ali, and Bluey
The Order of the Holy Paraclete, St Hilda's Priory, Whitby

'Let the Abbess appoint sisters on whose manner of life and character she can rely.'
From the Rule of St Benedict

There is a veritable chapter of cats connected with St Hilda's Priory and its neighbouring daughter houses. At the nearby retreat house of St Oswald's, Ali and Ozzie have made their home; at Beachcliff, a branch house of the order for retired sisters, Bluey is the resident cat; while Billy Boy lives at the Priory.

When I first met Ali and Ozzie, the cats of St Oswald's Retreat Centre, I must confess that their behaviour was not up to the standards of peace and reconciliation that one expects to find in a retreat house. That is to say, Ozzie was leaning over a parapet, raining down hefty blows onto Ali's head, who after a half-hearted attempt to retaliate, retired to the safety of a nearby tree, thereby illustrating the more conventional sense

HISTORY
St Hilda's Priory comprises two adjacent parts: Sneaton Castle, the original home of the order, and latterly a school run by the sisters; and the newer priory buildings, to the south. Surrounded by fields, and with inspiring views over the surrounding countryside, the Priory has a peaceful and serene atmosphere. The Priory also has two daughter houses, St Oswald's Retreat Centre and the nuns' retirement home, Beachcliff.

of 'retreat house'! The centre is a pleasing house with extensive and well-kept sloping woodland gardens. It was donated to the order by Lady Grimstone, and people come from all over to enjoy its peace and quiet. The chapel is the most striking part: Lady Grimstone was much taken with all things Celtic, and had it decorated with woad and oxblood.

Ozzie and Ali came to St Oswald's as 'millennium' kittens of barn pedigree. It was in a sense an invasion, as Sister Janet already had Tabitha, a calico cat who certainly didn't like kittens around. The two kittens were housed by Charles the gardener, in his shed: they had a heated bed, regular food, and a cat flap, through which they could clamber easily, but which thwarted

OPENING PAGE
Billy Boy – a friend to the older sisters
LEFT
Ozzie, in the woodlands of
St Oswald's
RIGHT
Bluey on the new log steps

Tabitha's efforts to invade and deliver a few well-aimed blows. So Ozzie and Ali issued challenges to Tabitha through the cat flap, safe in the knowledge that, as long as they didn't go out, Tabitha could not get at them.

In the meantime the two kittens were introduced into the household: the sisters took (reluctant) turns to take them to the vets for their injections. Each sister has been bitten at the vets by either Ozzie or Ali, and the vet is bitten by both of them on every visit. With the passing of time, Tabitha died, at the goodly age of 17 years, and Ozzie and Ali came out of cover to claim the territory, not without dispute, as a cat from down the valley tries to steal their food. But they did mellow a bit. Visitors to the centre, perhaps enjoying a gentle stroll around the grounds, are more than likely to come across Ozzie and Ali, passing each other perfectly amicably, though the next moment they may be locked in very unspiritual combat.

Back at St Hilda's Priory itself, Sneaton Castle, the original home of the order, is now a centre for conferences, run by the sisters, where day and residential groups come for a variety of activities – but the visitor is unlikely to come across Billy Boy, who has embraced the security of voluntary enclosure within the newer priory buildings. And with good reason too: this dark-haired, wide-eyed and slightly frail cat arrived about ten years ago, having been rescued by the Royal Society for the Prevention of Cruelty to Animals. For the sisters, a friendly cat was a

novelty. There had been another cat – an outdoor cat, with attitude. Difficult to approach, he lived his life in the grounds, away from human contact, preferring the shelter and protection of an enormous stack of cut wood. He did get a name – Woodpile Thomas – but eventually went his way to pastures unknown.

So Billy Boy is the first community cat: he has an array of sisters who attend to his various needs and wishes, and he reciprocates their attention – as befits a cat who understands where the good things of life come from. Sister Constance is his firmest friend and companion. When she is upstairs in her room adjacent to the infirmary, Billy Boy is there. When Sister Constance sits out in the rockery garden, enjoying the sun, Billy Boy comes out too. He often joins Sister Heather Francis, who gardens the rockery: Billy Boy sits and watches her gardening activities with curiosity, as his own attempts at gardening are discouraged. Billy Boy likes the quiet life: he appreciates being welcomed into community gatherings, and during the winter a special place is reserved for him by the log fire.

The life of Bluey is not so quiet. She lives with a group of retired sisters in the Priory's retirement home, Beachcliff, on the cliff tops of Whitby, and is a curious cat, a little delicate in health, who has the engaging habit of raising a forepaw in salutation. She shares the house with Bracken, a frightfully keen collie cross who had lived at the Priory for four years. Bluey arrived as a casualty, injured on a farm, and has a slight heart problem (although the vet always says that he can't hear her heart for all the purring). But despite her health issues, Bluey quickly established her primacy in the household: Bracken is forever trying to round everyone up for chapel and Bluey is happy to comply (and spends her time in chapel purring loudly), since in exchange she has taken over his bed. It's an arrangement that seems to suit both animals, for in practice they enjoy keeping each other company. And the sisters have constructed a little set of log steps, so that Bluey can step up to the back windows when she wants to come in.

LEFT
Ozzie and Ali stalk the gardens
BELOW
Ozzie gets ready to pounce on Ali

Acknowledgements

Society of St Francis, Alnmouth Friary – Agnes Brother Paschal and the community

Anglican Order of St Benedict, Alton – Millie Dom Giles Hill OSB, and the community

Poor Clare Monastery, Arkley – Inky Sister Francesca and the community

Anglican Order of St Benedict, Burford Priory – Blackie Father Stuart, Sister Mary Bernard and the community

The Order of Preachers, Blackfriars Cambridge – Leo Prior Aiden Nichols and the community

Community of the Holy Name, Derby – Tamar Sister Brenda and the community

The Community of St Mary at the Cross, Edgware – Felix, Tinker & Mrs Tiggy Dame Mary Catherine OSB and the community

Forde Abbey – Tabitha Twitchit & Tilly The Roper family and Hannah Galvin

Glenstal Abbey – Marmion & Hildegard Father Mark Tierney OSB and the community

St Monica's Priory, Hoxton – Jane Father Paul and Father Mark

The Iona Community, Iona Abbey – Splash Richard Sharples, Catherine, and the Iona community

Convent of the Poor Clares, Lynton – Oliver Sister Mary Magdalen and the community

Mottisfont Abbey – Murphy David Stone, Matt Wavell and Nick Coates

All Saints Convent, Oxford – Oscar Sister Mary Julian and the community

Holy Hill Hermitage, Skreen – Neri & Fiona The community

The Order of Buddhist Contemplatives, Throssel Hole Buddhist Abbey – Smudge The monks

The Ty Mawr Community, Society of the Sacred Cross – Mellagel, Miri & Merlin Sister Laurie and the community

The Society of Saint Margaret, Walsingham Priory – Bonnie Sister Jane Louise and the community

St Hilda's Priory, Whitby – Billy Boy, Ozzie & Ali, Bluey Sister Constance, Sister Janet Elizabeth, and their communities, and the retired sisters